I0190802

Our Father, Friend Of Little Children

Children's Object Lessons
Based On The Lord's Prayer

Wesley T. Runk

CSS Publishing Company, Inc.
Lima, Ohio

OUR FATHER, FRIEND OF LITTLE CHILDREN

Second Edition
Copyright © 1973, 1995 by
CSS Publishing Company, Inc.
Lima, Ohio

All rights reserved. No part of this publication may be reproduced, stored in a retrieval system, or transmitted in any form or by any means, electronic, mechanical, photocopying, recording, or otherwise, without the prior permission of the publisher. Inquiries should be addressed to: CSS Publishing Company, Inc., 517 South Main Street, P.O. Box 4503, Lima, Ohio 45802-4503.

ISBN 0-7880-0372-0   PRINTED IN U.S.A.

. . . for your Father knows what you need before you ask him. Pray then in this way . . .
— *Matthew 6:8b-9a*

Table Of Contents

Our Father Who Art In Heaven

Object: the flag (a Christian flag or the American flag)

Can you think of something that belongs to all of us? When I get up in the morning and look out of the window, I see a heaven and a sun, or some clouds that belong to us all. It is our sun and our heaven. Is there anything that you can think of that belongs to us all? *(Let them answer.)*

Some things belong to you and to me, and some things belong to us all. This means that you have your own teeth, your own clothes, your own house, and your own father and mother. Some things belong to you and some things belong to all of us.

I have something here this morning that belongs to all of us. *(Bring out the flag.)* This is our flag. It isn't your flag or my flag, but it's our flag and we love it because it belongs to all of us.

I want to tell you about someone who belongs to all of us. We all have one Father. Our Father is not someone whom you can see or touch, but He is the same for all of us. Our Father is in heaven and we call Him Our Father God. Each of us has a father, a different father, who lives with us and our mother. But this Father is different in many ways. Our Father God lives in Heaven, but He also lives with us on earth. He loves us all and not just one of us, nor does he love one of us more than the other. Our Father God called Jesus His Son, and told us that everyone who listened and believed in Jesus could be a brother or a sister to Jesus. Our Father God is not only someone to love us, but He also cares for us, makes sure that there is plenty of rain and sunshine, food to eat, places to stay, and other people to care about us. Our Father belongs to us all and cares for us all.

Some people wonder how Our Father God can do all of these things, and they ask questions about Him. We don't know all the answers to these questions, and we will never know all the answers until He chooses to tell us, but we are taught by Jesus that God is like a Father. He is interested in us and wants us to love the life that He gave us and enjoy it with others.

The wonderful thing about the Father God is that He does belong to us all, whether we are rich or poor, young or old, American or Russian, black or white, boy or girl. The Father God is a God for us all, just like the Flag belongs to all. We can't keep this Father in our home so that He cannot go other places, but while He is with us, He is also with everyone else. There is only one Father God but He belongs to us all.

This is why Jesus began His prayer with the words "Our Father" since He was teaching His disciples how to pray and He wanted them to know God as He knew God. I want you to learn about God the way that Jesus taught us, and so I am telling you that the first thing that you must remember is that God, our God who belongs to us all, is like a Father.

When you pray your special prayer today or tonight, I hope you remember to begin it with the words, "Our Father," and remember how wonderful those words are to all of us.

Hallowed Be Thy Name

Object: a microphone

How important is a name? How many of you have names? Does everyone here have a name? Is it possible that someone here does not have a name? All of you have names. I think that is wonderful. Do you have a good name? Is there any way that we could improve your name? Suppose that your name was Sally and we wanted to improve it. Would it make you any different if we called you LaSally or McSally? Would it make you any different if we called you by some other name like Big Sally or Happy Sally? I don't think that you would like that, do you? Changing your name doesn't change you, and people love you just the way you are.

I have something with me that will help explain what we are going to learn about today. How many of you know what I am talking about when I mention the word "microphone?" Everyone likes to use a microphone. Who can tell me what a microphone does when you use it? *(Let them answer.)* It makes your voice sound louder or bigger, doesn't it? Sure it does. Whenever you take a microphone in your hand and use it, and it is hooked up, you can make your voice be heard in many places. A microphone does something special with your voice.

The reason that I tell you this is because of some special words that are used in the Lord's Prayer. When Jesus taught

His disciples how to pray, He used the words, "Hallowed be Thy name." That means that we should do everything that we can to keep the name of God holy. Use God's name with great respect. When people talk about God they talk about Almighty God, Eternal God, Holy God and many other words that make God sound good and wonderful. God is not changed by those words. Your voice is not changed by the microphone. We use those words so that when we mention God's name we will remember that it is special. When you use the microphone you help people to hear you, but you do not help your voice. God stays the same no matter what you call Him. When we hallow God's Name we are helping to make Him special for us. We always want God to be special for us since He is such a wonderful God. God is already the biggest, smartest, happiest and most loving Person that we know, but when we pray to keep His name special to us we are reminding ourselves what we think about Him.

Turn on your microphone and your voice stays the same but many more people can hear you. Speak good things of God and God stays the same but He is something special to you. Jesus wanted us to hallow God's name so that God would be as special a Father to us as He was to Jesus.

The next time you see a microphone I hope that you will think of the wonderful words that we use and the wonderful feelings that we have about God, our Heavenly Father.

Thy Kingdom Come

Object: a large map, a globe, or an atlas with many maps

Jesus prayed that God's kingdom would come on earth as it is in heaven. What is God's kingdom? What is a kingdom? Today we would call it a nation or a city or a community. Have you ever looked at a big map or a globe of the earth and read the names of all the nations? There are many different sizes and shapes of nations. Some of them are great big like Russia or the United States and some of them are very tiny such as Israel or Liechtenstein. Nations are like cities; some of them are huge, great big, and some of them are very small. Jesus talks about God's nation as a special nation and He prays that God will make it here on earth just like it already is in heaven.

We are citizens of the United States, which means that we belong here and we serve our country. You can live in many places but to be a citizen is something special. When you are a citizen you are more than a visitor. A citizen pays taxes, votes in elections, and works to make his home a better place to live. In our land we have a president and congressmen, governors and mayors and councilmen. They are people that we elect to run our government in the best way they know how.

In God's nation, God is in charge. We don't elect God or choose Him in any special way because God is always in charge. His nation is perfect and there are no complaints. We don't pay any taxes in His nation either. Now, the kingdom or nation of God is not on the map or globe. You could look all day long and you would not find it anywhere on this map. God's nation is only for people after they die here on earth at the present time. But Jesus prayed in His prayer to the Father God that some day when the time was just right, God would make His nation here on earth in the same way that He has made it in heaven.

This is something that all Christians wait for and hope and pray for because when God chooses to build His nation on earth it will be a very special time. In God's kingdom or nation there is no war, hatred, sickness or worry. God's nation is a place of great beauty and all the people who live in it are ready to love and help each other.

We can't see God's kingdom or nation on a map or globe, but we know that it is alive and well. We also know that some day, according to Jesus, God is going to bring His kingdom to earth. Then we will all see it and know it and we will rejoice with everyone else that what we pray for is happening for everyone.

Thy Will Be Done On Earth,
As It Is In Heaven

Object: a rule book for a game like baseball or any sport that operates under the kind of management that an umpire or referee would have during a game

How many of you have gone to a baseball game lately and watched the umpire? Do you know who the umpire is? *(Let them answer.)* The umpire is the man in the blue suit or the fellow who is not dressed like the ball players. He acts like the boss. He tells you when you are safe or out, or when the pitch thrown is a ball or strike. The umpire is the boss, and when he knows all the rules and uses them correctly we have a good game. But can you imagine what it would be like if every umpire had his own rules? Suppose you were the umpire and you decided that it would make the game go faster if every ballplayer only got two strikes, and a team only got one out every inning? Another umpire might suggest that when you hit the ball you should run to third base instead of first base, and that home runs were outs and outs were home runs. Wouldn't that be a mess? The game would not be much fun either because everything would be mixed up so badly that no one could play. That's the reason that every umpire has a book like this. *(Hold up book.)* These are the rules of the game and it is the same if you play in Atlanta or Baltimore, Cincinnati or San Francisco. The umpire uses the same rules for every game and for every player. Then it is a good game and everyone loves to play baseball.

Our God has a way of playing the game also. In our prayer to the Father God we ask that he will do the same for us here on earth as He already does in heaven. We pray that His way will be our way, and that we will know what He wants to be done here on earth. God is kind of like the umpire except he never makes a mistake. God watches what we do and how we live our life and He loves the way that we enjoy His earth, and looks forward to the day that we will join Him in heaven. But sometimes we get things a little mixed up, and we try to play and live according to our rules rather than God's. It is kind of like playing ball with your friends and every friend has a different rule. God is not very happy when we mess up the rules. In the Bible the rules of heaven and earth are called the will of God. God's will is His way of doing things and having us do things. When we argue or twist or try to change God's will, we find ourselves in a real jam and it makes us pretty unhappy. That is why we pray that God will try to make us understand what He wants and that we will play and work with the rules that He wants us to use. God's will is a good thing, the best that there is, and it makes us happy when we use it. That's why we are asking God to show us the way so that we can have it as nice on earth as it is in heaven. Would it not be a wonderful thing to live on earth as the people do in heaven just like they play baseball the same in Cincinnati as they do in New York? God would like it that way and everybody who prays that God's will be done here as it is in heaven is asking for God to show him or her the way to live. God's will should be our will forever.

Give Us This Day Our Daily Bread

Object: a loaf of unsliced bread

If you could ask God for one thing that you thought He had, what would it be? Suppose you were in a big line of people who were going to ask God for something and you had plenty of time to think about what you wanted. What would you ask God for? Would you ask for a swimming pool in your backyard, or an airplane to fly around the world, or a brand new ball and bat? What do you think that God has something of that you would want if you only had the chance to ask? When Jesus prayed to His Father in Heaven He asked for something that He thought was really important, and He taught all of His disciples to ask for the same thing. Do you know what Jesus asked the Father to give Him? *(Let them answer.)*
Jesus asked for bread. *(Hold up bread.)* Can you imagine that? Jesus asked the Father for bread. He didn't ask for anything else, just bread. Not only that, but His disciples began praying for bread, and all of the people since, like you and me, pray that the Father will give them bread. Do you remember the place in the Lord's Prayer where we pray, "Give us this day our daily bread"? We pray that lots of times. No one ever prays every day for a swimming pool or an airplane or even a ball and bat but they do pray for bread, daily bread. Do you know why? *(Let them answer.)*

First, bread is important. We need bread to live and everybody eats bread of one sort or another. But that is not the reason. When Jesus asked for bread He did so because He meant that bread stood for everything that we need to live. Bread is like a symbol. Bread stands for clothes and houses and all other kinds of food. When you ask God to take care of the things that you need every day you are asking for a lot and you are getting a lot. Just think of the things that God gives you to live with every day. Since you eat bread every day Jesus decided that bread could stand for everything else, even the things that you don't eat every day, but that you do need. Ask God for green beans or cheese or the roof on the house to be fixed or shoes to wear on your feet or a coat to keep you warm if you want to, but Jesus just asked God for daily bread and He knew that God would give to us whatever we needed. It is wonderful that God knows what we need and still lets us ask for it. He could just put them on, in, or over us, but instead He lets us be a partner and ask Him for the things that we need.

The next time you see a loaf of bread you will remember that Jesus used it as a symbol for all the things that we need and you will then remember that God gives us everything and that everything comes from God.

And Forgive Us Our Trespasses, As We Forgive Those Who Trespass Against Us

Object: a NO TRESPASSING sign

Have you ever been some place that you were not supposed to be? Have you ever crossed a busy street when you were not supposed to, or gone into someone's yard where children are not allowed to play, and then remembered that this was going to get you into trouble? If any of those things have ever happened to you, then you know what an awful feeling it is to be somewhere that you are not supposed to be. I had a neighbor who had a sign in his yard that told everyone to stay out. His sign looked something like this: *(Hold up the NO TRESPASSING sign.)* Can you read this? It says NO TRESPASSING. Do you know what that means? It means that you had better not come into the yard or he will cause you a lot of trouble.

In our Lord's Prayer the word trespasses is used. It means something like the sign is trying to say. The word trespasses means sins. It means that when we sin we have done something or gone somewhere or thought something that we should not have. If the man in the yard caught you after he put up his sign, he might call the police or come out and give you a bawling out, or tell your parents what you did and ask them to punish you. When we commit a sin against God we know that something should be done to us. We expect God to punish us in a manner that we will remember, so that we will not do it again. But in the prayer that Jesus teaches us to pray, we are asking that God will forgive our trespasses or sins and forget all about it.

Of course Jesus knew that anyone who wanted God to forgive his sins would want to forgive the sins that other people had committed against him. God will forgive your trespasses, your sins, if you will forgive the things that other people do to you. If someone calls you a name that you don't like, plays with your friend and doesn't allow you to play, or takes something that belongs to you and doesn't give it back, they are trespassing against you. These and all the other things like it that hurt your feelings are the things that you must forgive. They are wrong and they should not be done, but you must forgive them. Then when you go to God and ask Him to forgive you for your sins or trespasses He will be able to say, "Since you have forgiven all of those who sinned against you I am glad to forgive you."

We know when we are sinning against God and God knows when we are doing it that it is a sin, but God would much rather forgive you than punish you. Remember that your friends feel the same way that you do. They would rather be forgiven than punished, and have their trespasses forgotten. So take your trespasses to God after you have forgiven the trespasses of your friends and everyone, including you, will be happy.

And Lead Us Not Into Temptation

Object: box of chocolates, potato chips, popcorn, etc.

Do you ever think that someday you will be on a diet? You know what a diet is, don't you? *(Let them answer.)* That's right, a diet is when you can't eat the things that you like the most, and you can eat as much as you want of things that you don't like. How many of you like hamburgers with lots of things on them, potatoes with gravy, chocolate candy, potato chips, ice cream, soda pop, and things like that? You can't have any of that on your diet but you can have spinach, brussel sprouts, radishes, celery, fish, green peppers and lettuce. How many of you like those foods? Not very many of you. Some day when you get overweight you will have to go on one of those special diets. Of course, not all of the people are extra heavy, but the ones who are not are tempters. Do you know what a tempter is? *(Let them answer.)* A tempter is a skinny person who likes to walk around with a box of chocolates, some potato chips, a bottle of pop and other goodies, eating them and asking fat people if they would like to have some of the things they are carrying. The fat person is doing his best to stay on the diet and keep away from things like that so that he will lose weight. When the tempter is around it is easy to give in and eat what you should not eat and then the diet is lost. Woe is me when I give in to the tempter.

That is in fun but the real tempter is not so funny. When we pray to God to keep us from temptation we are praying that God will protect us from the devil. The devil is always trying to trick us into thinking that what is wrong is all right this time. The devil can make the worst thing in the world look good, so good that we can hardly resist it. That is the way he works. When we pray to God for His help we are asking Him to help us stay away from the devil and the things that he does to us. The devil can make us think that it is all right this time for us to tell a lie or take something that doesn't belong to us. We pray to our Father in heaven that He will stay close to us and not allow the tricky devil to get close to us and tempt us.

Temptation is a terrible thing because it is so confusing. What is wrong looks right and what is right looks wrong. We need God to help us make decisions for what is right and to keep us away from the tempters.

The next time you see someone take a big piece of candy or eat two large bowls of ice cream and tell you that they shouldn't eat either one, then you can remember the story of the tempter. When you see that, you can also remember that we must stay away from the devil and all of his tricks, and instead listen to God and be filled with goodness.

But Deliver Us From Evil

Object: a newspaper, some flowers, dry cleaning or any item
that is normally delivered

Some of the nicest work in the world is delivering. Do you
know anyone who delivers something to you? *(Let them answer.)* Good. Almost everyone has something delivered to him
like a newspaper, packages, pizza or on special occasions some
flowers. I know that I am very pleased with the boy who
delivers my newspaper every night. It doesn't make any differ-
ence if it rains or snows or if the sunshine is blistering hot,
the newspaper is always delivered to my house.

Have you thought about the word "deliver" and what it
means? Just think for a moment with me about that word and
you will see how important it is to have something delivered.
What does the word mean to you? *(Let them answer.)* When
you deliver something it means that you have gotten it in one
place and taken it to another. The newspaper boy or the florist
gets his paper or flowers from one place and takes it to your
house and we call it delivering. Only because he brings it does
it arrive. If he did not deliver it you would have to go to the
newspaper office every day and pick up a newspaper or to a
flower shop and buy your flowers. Of course you could have
your own flower garden or your own bakery and make or grow
all of the things yourself. But if you did that you would not

have the time to do your job or any of the other things that you like to do so well. We are very grateful for the people who deliver things to us.

The prayer that Jesus taught us also talks about delivering, only Jesus prayed that God would deliver us. Just like the paper boy delivers the paper so God delivers you and me. That must mean that God gets us one place and takes us to some other place.

Can you imagine where God is delivering us? Where is He getting us and where is He taking us? *(Let them answer.)* That's right, God is going to deliver us to heaven, but where is He getting us? The Bible says that God is taking us away from evil. There are evil places that boys and girls and moms and dads can get into and we can't get away by ourselves. God promises to deliver us from the bad places to the good place of heaven. God delivers us and we are so glad. That is why Jesus taught us to make that part of our prayer to the Father. "Deliver us from evil," Jesus prayed, and told us all to include it in our prayer. We are so glad that God answers our prayer and is ready to get us when we need to get away from the bad things and take us to the good place called heaven.

Delivering is fun and it is work, but for God it is something that He does for everyone who asks and He does it gladly. Ask God to deliver you and you can live some day with Him in heaven and you will never have to worry about being left where it is evil.

For Thine Is The Kingdom,
And The Power, And The Glory
For Ever And Ever. Amen.

Object: some banners or flags to wave

Have you ever been some place where the people were so happy that they wanted to shout and cheer and tell everyone else how good they felt? I love to go to a parade and see some big hero like the President or some other great leader and stand in a big crowd and cheer with my loud voice and wave a flag or banner in the air. The big hero may not even know that I am there but I like to go and show how much I appreciate the good things he is doing.

The end of the Lord's Prayer is a little like this. Since we are so glad to have talked with God and told Him about all the things that we need, we now just want to thank Him as much as we can and tell Him what a great God He really is. If we all had some banners we might take them at the end of the prayer where we say, "For thine is the kingdom, and the power, and the glory for ever and ever. Amen," and just wave them and clap our hands for joy. That is the way I feel when I finish praying the prayer, because now I know that everything that I need is being taken care of and I am safe in the hands of God, and know that He knows who I am and what I need. God is like the greatest hero ever, only better, and He knows us. Great heroes do not know very many of us, but God knows everyone and knows them better than their best friends do.

23

That is the reason we feel so great when we finish talking to God. We say, "Thine is the kingdom, power and glory." That is especially why we say, "Amen," because we mean that as far as we are concerned we are willing to leave it all up to God to see that everything turns out okay. Can you imagine what it might be like to stand in front of God someday and wave a banner and tell Him how much you love Him and what a great job He did for you? Well, that is what we are trying to do with the last words of our Lord's Prayer. Glory be to God and praise Him forever for the marvelous things that He has done for all of us every day of our lives. Amen, Amen, and Amen.

www.ingramcontent.com/pod-product-compliance
Lightning Source LLC
Chambersburg PA
CBHW071810020426
42331CB00008B/2455

* 9 7 8 0 7 8 8 0 0 3 7 2 1 *